Forms for Helping the ADHD Child

By Lawrence E. Shapiro, Ph.D.

Childswork/Childsplay
Secaucus, New Jersey

Forms for Helping the ADHD Child
By Lawrence E. Shapiro, Ph.D.

© 1995 by Childswork/Childsplay, LLC, a subsidiary of Genesis Direct, Inc., 100 Plaza Drive, Secaucus, NJ 07094. 1-800-962-1141. All rights reserved.
Printed in the United States of America.

ISBN# 1-882732-39-1

TABLE OF CONTENTS

Introduction

There is a tremendous amount of information available regarding the psycho-educational treatment of the ADHD child. When looking for information to help an ADHD child, the professional mental health clinician or educator is faced with several hundred books, videotapes, workbooks, and even storybooks for children on the meaning of ADHD. And yet there still seems to be a lack of practical and simple books on treatment.

This book consists of forms covering a wide range of approaches used to help the ADHD child. The forms in this book emphasize behavioral strategies, since research studies have made it clear that these are invariably the best approaches. The forms are simple and to the point and can be photocopied from the book and used to treat ADHD children. This book does not detail the theory or procedures behind the forms, but rather assumes that the professional will have gathered that information from one of the many popular sources (many of which are listed in the Bibliography).

While this book was designed to provide highly practical and concise tools for professionals working with ADHD children, its simplicity does not mitigate the need for an in-depth understanding of this childhood problem. On the contrary, the techniques chosen to help an ADHD child should be carefully weighed and thoroughly understood before they are undertaken, so as to avoid a trial-and-error approach. In most cases, a combination of techniques aimed at different aspects of the problem will be most appropriate.

It is hoped that the forms in this book will be used to make the clinician's job a little bit easier, in providing quick tools to assess, treat, and monitor the progress of the ADHD child.

#1 Activities Schedule

Many ADHD children have difficulty in being at the right place at the right time. The **Activities Schedule** can be used to help the child remember and perform the important independent activities of the child's daily life, including homework, chores, and other responsibilities. Rather than just listing difficult activities, the adult might wish to also list pleasurable activities like watching TV or playing, and neutral activities such as getting ready for bed. This will help give the child a sense of the importance of completing tasks on time.

Activities Schedule

DAILY SCHEDULE

Name_____

DAY:_____

DATE:_____

TIME	TASK OR ACTIVITY	CHECK WHEN DONE (ADD COMMENTS IF NOT DONE)

#2 Anger Thermometer

Self-calming techniques include a variety of relaxation training techniques, designed to help children lower their body-arousal state when they feel that they are likely to act out aggressively. Children prone to anger become hypervigilant to their surroundings when they are aroused, and typically respond to what they perceive as hostile remarks and nonverbal cues that other children don't see.

To reduce the dysfunctional expression of anger and aggressiveness, children can be taught to recognize what makes them angry and inhibit their arousal. Children can be taught to identify situations in which they are likely to feel "wound up," and to recognize the internal and external cues associated with that state.

The **Anger Thermometer** can help children to identify the people, places, and things that raise them to the "boiling point" as well as those that help them calm down.

The Anger Thermometer

It is important to understand what makes you "hot" and what "cools" you down. Write in the people, places, and things that make you feel mad or calm.

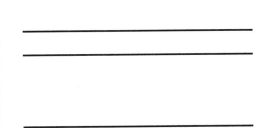

BOILING
OVER

STEAMING
HOT

WARM

98.6
(NORMAL)

COOL

COLD

FRIGID

PEOPLE, PLACES, THINGS

_____
_____

_____
_____

_____
_____

_____
_____

_____
_____

_____
_____

_____
_____

#3 Antecedents & Consequences of Problem Behaviors

Behavioral psychology assumes that most problematic behaviors are preceded by events that trigger a particular behavior and are followed by events that reinforce the behavior. These events, or antecedents, may often be modified in order to prevent the problematic behavior from occurring and being reinforced.

The **Antecedents and Consequences of Problem Behaviors** chart can be used to help identify things that trigger and/or reinforce the problematic behavior. Observation periods should take place at times when the child is likely to have problems, for 15- to 30-minute periods. Observation should occur for at least a week, in most cases, in order to see a pattern.

Antecedents & Consequences of Problem Behaviors

Name of Child: _____   Date: _____

Person Filling Out Chart: _____

Relation to Child: _____

Observations			
Describe the Problem	What Happened Just Before the Problem Behavior?	What Happened Just After the Problem Behavior?	Time Period

#4 Behavior Discipline Chart

This chart can be used to record incidents of misbehavior, the results of the misbehavior, the disciplinary consequences, and the reaction of the child to the discipline. The chart can be filled in by the parent or teacher on a daily basis, for at least a week, to see patterns of misbehavior and the results of specific discipline.

Behavior Discipline Chart

Date and Time	Misbehavior	Result of Misbehavior	Disciplinary Consequences	Reaction of Child

#5 Behavior Self-Rating

One of the most important goals for all behavioral programs is to teach the child self-observation skills. The **Behavior Self-Rating Scale** can be used to help children assess their own behaviors. The column at the far right would then be completed by the parent or someone who knew the child well. This column would be used to assess the accuracy of the child's answers.

Behavior Self-Rating Scale

Name of Child_____ Date_____

Check the box that best describes your behavior today.

Behavior	None of the time	Some of the time	All of the time	Agree Yes/No
I am messy.				
I like to play sports.				
I have a problem paying attention in class.				
I am well-liked by my classmates.				
I have problems making friends.				
I read difficult books.				
I have problems completing my assignments.				
I eat fruits and vegetables.				
I have problems following rules.				
I get in fights with other kids.				
I exercise.				
I am often late for class.				
I do my chores on time.				
I get in trouble for my behavior.				

Comments:

_____
_____
_____
_____

#6 Behavioral Contract

Behavioral contracts are an effective method for getting children to work on specific goals for specific rewards. They are most successful for behaviors that the child has not been able to accomplish in the past, but is currently doing consistently. Behavioral contracts should not be used if the task or goal is very difficult for the child, because they do not give the ADHD child the frequent reinforcement that is needed to change an old behavior or learn a new one.

The **Behavioral Contract** should be filled out by the child and adults together and signed by all parties involved. The goal must be very clear and the reward should only be given if the goal is accomplished.

Behavoral Contract

I, _____, agree to do the following:

(name of child)

.

1. _____
2. _____
3. _____
4. _____
5. _____

that I will do these will earn me one of the following rewards:

Each period of _____

1. _____
2. _____
3. _____
4. _____
5. _____

I understand that if I do not complete these responsibilities I will not earn the rewards on this contract.

I agree to try to fulfill this contract to the best of my abilities.

Signed,   Date

child: _____   _____

parent: _____   _____

teacher: _____   _____

13

#7 Childhood Motivation Checklist

The majority of ADHD children are placed on a reward system at some time. To be effective, the rewards children earn must have real value to them. But even rewards with significant value may lose their luster after a few weeks, and the child's behavior will plateau. This can be avoided if the child has a list of possible rewards, and new rewards, are assigned frequently.

The **Childhood Motivation Checklist** is designed to determine which kinds of things are most motivating to the child. The child is asked to rate the rewards on a 1-5 scale with 1=worst and 5=best. Rewards with a "five" rating should be used in the token economy program. Space is also given for the child to suggest rewards with a "5" rating. It is up to the adult to then decide how many points must be earned for these motivating rewards.

Childhood Motivation Checklist

What motivates you?

Directions: Rate the following rewards from 1 to 5 (1=worst 5=best).
Add more "best" rewards if you can.

1. _____ Cookie
2. _____ Extra half hour of TV
3. _____ Time with parent doing whatever I want (that doesn't cost anything)
4. _____ Special meal
5. _____ Trip to the zoo
6. _____ A cassette tape or CD
7. _____ Extra time on computer
8. _____ Extra time on video games
9. _____ Rent a video
10. _____ Ice cream cone
11. _____ Trip to a video arcade
12. _____ Trip to play miniature golf
13. _____ Pizza for dinner
14. _____ Comic book
15. _____ Swimming
16. _____ Bake cookies with a parent
17. _____ New markers/crayons
18. _____ Play a sport with a parent (basketball, bowling, etc.)
19. _____ Parent reads a story
20. _____ Make-your-own sundae
21. _____ Trading cards (Magic, baseball, etc.)
22. _____ Stay up a half-hour later
23. _____ Kid's magazine
24. _____ Paperback book
25. _____ Movie
26. _____ Extra hour of TV
27. _____ Time with a parent of your choice
28. _____ A meal at a fast food restaurant
29. _____ A trip to the library
30. _____ _____
31. _____ _____
32. _____ _____
33. _____ _____
34. _____ _____
35. _____ _____

15

#8 The Children's Self-Control Checklist

DIRECTIONS:

The Children's Self-Control Checklist was designed to shed light on how self-control mechanisms affect some of the most difficult-to-treat childhood disorders, including ADHD, Conduct Disorders, and Defiant Disorders, as well as less serious forms of uncooperativeness and impulsivity. From a treatment perspective, it is important to identify the pervasiveness of the problem across different settings, the degree that the problem affects the child's functioning, and the degree to which the adults can reasonably expect change given the developmental age and characterological make-up of the child.

This checklist is intended to give the professional educator or mental health professional a quick way to identify problems in self-control in four important areas: control of affect, control of behaviors, cognitive control, and moral development.

Self-control, like other personality variables, has both a common meaning and a psychological meaning. Today, particularly with the prevalence of the diagnosis of Attention Deficit Disorder with Hyperactivity (ADHD), we commonly refer to self-control as the opposite of impulsivity. But overweight children, for example, may lack self-control when it comes to eating. Or a bright, introspective child, who has temper tantrums when she is frustrated, may also lack specific self-control mechanisms.

For the purpose of clinical treatment, self-control can be broken down into four basic constructs related to a child's expression of affect, behavior, cognitive style and degree of moral development. The control of affect refers to the degree to which the child is able to control his/her inappropriate emotions in an age-appropriate and socially-appropriate manner.

Behavioral control includes compliant and cooperative behaviors, control of impulses, and self-regulatory behaviors. By cognitive style, we refer to the degree to which the child uses age-appropriate cognitive processes to adapt to and affect his environment, including such cognitive skills as problem-solving, planning ahead, organizing, decision-making and so on. Moral development refers to the degree to which the child sees the value of developing self-control as it relates to his concern over how his behavior affects others. The highest form of this area of self-control has to do with having an orientation towards others (i.e., altruism) rather than towards the self.

Each item within the four components of the checklist suggests specific treatment goals, as well as places where intervention with the child can occur. If possible, a multi modal approach should be used in planning a treatment program, intervening in all four areas simultaneously. This approach assures that both the child's weaknesses and strengths will be addressed. The Children's Self-Control Checklist can be used as a way of gathering information about a child's self-control, as a pre- and post treatment checklist, or as a way to consider different treatment interventions. The higher the score, the more self-control skills the child has learned.

The checklist was developed primarily for use with children ages 5 to 12.

DIRECTIONS: The Children's Self-Control Checklist has been developed to aid in assessing specific problems in self-control in the home and in the school. The checklist may be filled out by the clinician who interviews the primary care-taker and the primary teacher, or it may be filled out by the parent and the teacher directly. In the latter case, information supplied by the first respondent should be covered with a sheet of paper so as not to influence the rating of the second respondent.

Please circle the number that best describes each statement.
1=False   2=Sometimes True   3=Always True   DK=Don't Know

	Home				School			

I. Control of Affects (Emotions)

1. The child can name 5 to 10 different emotions and tell of a time he/she has had these emotions.
1 2 3 DK   1 2 3 DK

2. The child can recognize that different emotions are appropriate in different situations.
1 2 3 DK   1 2 3 DK

3. The child can name three people to talk to about his/her feelings.
1 2 3 DK   1 2 3 DK

4. The child can recognize the effect of his/her emotions on others.
1 2 3 DK   1 2 3 DK

5. The child can name three strategies to calm down when he/she is angry or upset.
1 2 3 DK   1 2 3 DK

6. The child can name three things that might happen if he/she loses his/her temper.
1 2 3 DK   1 2 3 DK

7. The child can recognize physical cues that signal a loss of control, such as rapid breathing, sweating, body tension, etc.
1 2 3 DK   1 2 3 DK

8. The child can use relaxation techniques to calm himself/herself down.
1 2 3 DK   1 2 3 DK

9. The child can recognize the emotional states of others by nonverbal cues.
1 2 3 DK   1 2 3 DK

II. Behavioral Control

10. The child cooperates with positive behavioral programs to change his/her behavior, such as a point system.
1 2 3 DK   1 2 3 DK

11. The child will cooperate with negative discipline techniques such as time-out.
1 2 3 DK   1 2 3 DK

12. The child does not bother others when they are busy.
1 2 3 DK   1 2 3 DK

13. The child waits to be asked to play.
1 2 3 DK   1 2 3 DK

14. The child can do one thing at a time.
1 2 3 DK   1 2 3 DK

15. The child waits for his/her turn to talk.
1 2 3 DK   1 2 3 DK

16. The child waits for answers to his/her questions.
1 2 3 DK   1 2 3 DK

17. The child can wait in a line without disturbing others.
1 2 3 DK   1 2 3 DK

18. The child can stop himself/herself in the face of temptation.
1 2 3 DK   1 2 3 DK

19. The child sits quietly for extended periods of time.
1 2 3 DK   1 2 3 DK

20. The child can ignore verbal provocation.
1 2 3 DK   1 2 3 DK

	Home				School			
21. The child can ignore physical provocation.	1	2	3	DK	1	2	3	DK
22. The child has developed a strategy and a back-up plan to deal with provocation.	1	2	3	DK	1	2	3	DK
23. The child follows complicated directions (e.g., multiple directions or directions where an activity occurs in the future).	1	2	3	DK	1	2	3	DK
24. The child can identify people or situations that commonly lead to behavioral problems.	1	2	3	DK	1	2	3	DK
25. The child avoids people or situations that can lead to behavioral problems.	1	2	3	DK	1	2	3	DK
26. The child does chores and other regularly scheduled activities without prompting.	1	2	3	DK	1	2	3	DK
27. The child completes independent work without prompting.	1	2	3	DK	1	2	3	DK
28. The child can name at least three situations where self-control is important.	1	2	3	DK	1	2	3	DK
29. The child can self-monitor his/her own behavior.	1	2	3	DK	1	2	3	DK

III. Cognitive Control

	Home				School			
30. The child can verbalize a statement that will help him/her keep control.	1	2	3	DK	1	2	3	DK
31. The child can work independently on a task for the same amount of time as his/her peers or use aids to help him/her stay on task.	1	2	3	DK	1	2	3	DK
32. The child can make age-appropriate decisions about important matters (e.g., homework, health issues, etc.).	1	2	3	DK	1	2	3	DK
33. The child can plan ahead for short periods of time (two hours or less).	1	2	3	DK	1	2	3	DK
34. The child can name two possible consequences to his/her behaviors.	1	2	3	DK	1	2	3	DK

(Items 35-41 apply only to children ages 8 and older)

	Home				School			
35. The child can use a planner or organizer to follow a daily schedule.	1	2	3	DK	1	2	3	DK
36. The child can plan for activities one day in advance.	1	2	3	DK	1	2	3	DK
37. The child can plan activities for the week or longer.	1	2	3	DK	1	2	3	DK
38. The child can list tasks that must be accomplished and prioritize them.	1	2	3	DK	1	2	3	DK
39. The child can come up with age-appropriate alternative solutions to a problem.	1	2	3	DK	1	2	3	DK
40. The child can compare alternative solutions to a problem.	1	2	3	DK	1	2	3	DK
41. The child can use a watch or clock to monitor his/her activities.	1	2	3	DK	1	2	3	DK

IV. Moral Development

	Home				School			
42. The child obeys explicit rules that are directly stated or written down.	1	2	3	DK	1	2	3	DK
43. The child obeys implicit rules that are not directly stated, but expected of a child his/her age.	1	2	3	DK	1	2	3	DK

	Home				School			
44. The child recognizes the difference between "right" and "wrong" behavior.	I	2	3	DK	I	2	3	DK
45. The child does not take things that don't belong to him/her.	I	2	3	DK	I	2	3	DK
46. The child is truthful about his/her mistakes, accidents, or misdeeds.	I	2	3	DK	I	2	3	DK
47. The child apologizes when confronted with a misdeed.	I	2	3	DK	I	2	3	DK
48. The child keeps his/her promises.	I	2	3	DK	I	2	3	DK
49. The child is concerned about the approval of adults.	I	2	3	DK	I	2	3	DK
50. The child is concerned about the approval of his/her peers.	I	2	3	DK	I	2	3	DK
51. The child shows concern for other people's feelings.	I	2	3	DK	I	2	3	DK
52. The child is considerate or thoughtful towards the important people in his/her life.	I	2	3	DK	I	2	3	DK
53. The child is concerned about the general welfare of others he/she doesn't know.	I	2	3	DK	I	2	3	DK

Total _____   Total _____

Notes

19

#9 The Children's Self-Image Scale

Sometimes, mental health and educational professionals are so concerned about an ADHD child's behavior that they forget the importance of having a good self-concept. Other times, adults misinterpret the exuberance of an ADHD child for happiness, forgetting that some children mask their depression through over-activity. The **Children's Self-Image Scale** will help determine a child's self-concept. The higher the score, the higher the child's self-esteem. Normally this form would be read to the child by the counselor or teacher, but it also could be filled in directly by an older child.

Children's Self-Image Scale

Directions: Answer the following questions according to how you *really* feel.

0=Never
1=Sometimes
2=Always

1. _____ I am smart.
2. _____ I help others.
3. _____ I am good at sports.
4. _____ I am good in school.
5. _____ Kids like me.
6. _____ My teacher thinks I'm a good student.
7. _____ I am a leader.
8. _____ I am happy.
9. _____ My parents love me.
10. _____ I tell the truth.
11. _____ I like the way I look.
12. _____ I am healthy.
13. _____ Kids tell me their secrets.
14. _____ I like to be with other kids.
15. _____ People say I have a nice smile.
16. _____ Kids pick me first to be on their team.
17. _____ I am good at games.
18. _____ I like to play with kids my age.
19. _____ I have just about everything I need to be happy.
20. _____ I sleep well at night.
21. _____ I like to talk on the phone with other kids.
22. _____ I have lots of things to do on weekends.
23. _____ I am always busy after school.
24. _____ I do well on tests.
25. _____ I think I will have a good job when I grow up.

#10 The Children's Stress Scale

Stress is an often-overlooked factor in understanding the mental health of children. The **Children's Stress Scale** was designed to provide a qualitative measure not only of the stress factors that affect children, but also of their resources and ability to cope with the stress. To obtain a qualitative Stress Factor score, subtract the child's "resources" from the sum of his/her external and internal stressors. This Stress Factor may have significant implications for treatment.

Children's Stress Scale

Version 1.0
A Rating Scale to Measure Stress in Children and Their Ability to Cope with It

Few people will disagree that stress is an important issue in the lives of children. Just as with adults, it is a factor in both their physical and mental health. Stress may underlie a wide assortment of common physical complaints, including headaches, stomachaches, and fatigue, and may be a factor in chronic illnesses such as asthma and ulcers.

Stress can also be a predisposing factor in a range of psychological problems, including, but not limited to, depression, academic underachievement, anxiety disorders, drug and alcohol abuse, aggression and so on. But a child under stress may not necessarily be symptomatic. In many cases, severe stress can exist in children at a subclinical level, and its toll may not show up until adolescence or even adulthood.

Identifying and understanding the stress that a child is experiencing is only half the story. What is equally important is a child's ability to cope with stress. There are many factors that can be important in how children can cope, including their inner resources, the support of their immediate family, and other environmental factors (such as school, friends, and community involvement). Therefore, no two children will experience stress exactly the same way.

The Children's Stress Scale is an attempt to qualitatively measure the stress factors in a child's life as well as that child's resources in handling stress. The Children's Stress Scale was primarily designed to provide the user with intervention strategies; helping parents and professionals reduce stress and increase a child's ability to handle it. Most importantly, we hope that this scale can be an aid in making children aware of stress and helping them develop lifelong habits in dealing with it.

Instructions

The Children's Stress Scale consists of two parts – stress factors and coping mechanisms. If you feel, because of specific factors unique to each child, that a statement should be rated higher or lower, you should feel free to add or subtract five points from that statement. Note adjustments in the column at the right with either a plus or minus sign.

Since it is impossible to list every situation or factor that affect a child's life, the adult filling out this scale should add additional statements as he/she sees fit under the section marked *Other Stress Factors*.

Give each Stress Factor a numerical value according to the following scale and add that number into the total Stress Score:

30	Traumatic stress factors
25	Highly significant, but not necessarily traumatic stress
20	Significant stress factors which may vary according to individual circumstances
15	Normal, but intense stress in the child's life or the family
10	Normal, but cumulative stress in the child's life
5	Low, persistent stress factors

Give each additional Coping Mechanism a score according to the following scale and add that number into the total Coping Mechanism Score:

4	Inner Resources
3	Family
2	Community

Part I: Identifying Stress Factors

Circle the number next to the statements below that describe the child you are rating.

Score   **Adjustments**
                                                                                 (+ or - 5 pts)

30   The child's parents have been separated/divorced for a period of less than one year.   _____

30   The child's parents are actively fighting over a significant issue in the child's life (this could be a custody or visitation issue, but it could also include such issues as where to go to school, a discipline issue, etc.).   _____

30   A member of the child's immediate family has died within the past year (father, mother, sibling, or a significant other with whom the child spent more than ten hours a week).   _____

30   The child has experienced a natural disaster within the past 12 months, including: fire, earthquake, flooding, and so on.   _____

30   The child frequently uses "drugs" including alcohol, illegal substances, as well as cigarettes, and the abuse of vitamins, diet pills, and so on.   _____

25   The child's family has moved more than 100 miles away.   _____

25   The child has had to switch schools.   _____

25   The child has experienced a recent separation, with limited contact, from one parent due to military duty, job relocation, or other external factors.   _____

25   One or both of the child's parents has remarried within the past year (this situation can be more stressful depending on many factors including the presence of step siblings, the child's relationship with the step parent, and so on).   _____

25   The child has experienced a prolonged illness (more than 1 month) and/or hospitalization.   _____

20   The child *occasionally* uses "drugs" including alcohol and illegal substances, as well as cigarettes, and the abuse of vitamins, diet pills, and so on.   _____

20   The family income has been substantially reduced in the past six months.   _____

20	The child is experiencing a prolonged period of difficulties in school.	_____
20	The child is experiencing significant problems with his/her peers, including, but not limited to: prolonged teasing or harassment, social ostracism, aggression toward or from peers, etc.	_____
20	The child perceives that he/she is significantly different than his/her close peers (due to physical differences, ethnic or racial differences, language differences, learning differences, and so on).	_____
20	One or more of a child's parents has a significant or chronic physical or mental illness.	_____
15	The parents of a child are experiencing prolonged and obvious problems including: frequent quarreling, problems at work, problems with relatives, health-related problems, etc.	_____
15	The child is entering a new school as part of his/her normal school career (e.g., preschool to elementary school, elementary to middle school, etc.)	_____
15	The child is in a disadvantaged environment (e.g., the family's income is below the poverty line and/or the child is exposed to significant social problems).	_____
15	Expectations for the child are significantly unrealistic concerning his/her innate abilities.	_____
10	The child is having a significant reaction to local or world events (e.g., The Persian Gulf War caused fears and anxiety in a significant number of the nation's children. Local or regional news about violence may have a similar effect on some children.).	_____
10	The child's week is "over scheduled," so that nearly every day he/she is running from one activity to another (a "hurried" child).	_____
5	There is a general lack of organization and scheduling in the household.	_____
5	The child does not have a nutritious, well-balanced diet.	_____
5	The child is entering a new school year.	_____
5	The child watches television and/or plays video games for more than two hours a day.	_____
5	The child is exposed to long periods of high-decibel noise.	_____

Other Stress Factors (please fully describe and enter an appropriate numerical rating of 30, 25, 20, 15, 10, or 5)

_____

_____

_____

_____

Total Score _____
Plus or Minus Adjustments _____
Final Stress Factors Score _____

Part II: Coping Mechanisms

Circle the numbers by the statements that accurately describe the child whom you are rating from an age-appropriate perspective.

Score | **Adjustments (+ or - 5 pts)**

Inner Resources:

4	The child readily communicates his/her feelings.	_____
4	The child has hobbies or interests (other than schoolwork) that he/she spends time with each week.	_____
4	The child has excellent study and organizational skills.	_____
4	The child actively seeks out adult help when needed.	_____

4	The child actively seeks out peer help for support when needed.	____
4	The child has a resilient personality and even-tempered disposition.	____
4	The child adapts particularly well to transitions.	____
4	The child has an exceptional drive towards independence.	____

Family:

3	The child has specific time each week to spend with one or both parents.	____
3	The child sees his/her extended family (aunt/uncle, cousins, grandparents, etc.) at least once a week.	____
3	The child has a close relationship with one or more siblings.	____
3	The family has weekly "rituals" of events that it does as a unit (e.g., a religious ritual, playing a game every Friday night, etc.).	____
3	The family has specific and regularly-scheduled meetings to talk about family issues and concerns.	____
3	The child has regularly-scheduled chores or other responsibilities.	____
3	The child lives in an "organized household" where events are planned and scheduled, TV time is monitored, meals occur at a regular time, etc.	____

Community:

2	The child has one "best friend," with whom he/she spends some time almost every day.	____
2	The child has a group of friends with whom he/she shares activities at least once a week.	____
2	The child participates regularly in a religious school or service.	____
2	The child experiences frequent success in school.	____
2	The child has frequent successful experiences in the community (e.g. sports, clubs, etc.).	____

Other Coping Mechanisms (please fully describe and enter an appropriate numerical rating):

_____

_____

_____

_____

Total Coping Score _____

Scoring

To obtain a combined total score, you should subtract the score for Part II (Coping Mechanisms) from the score for Part I (Stress Factors). You should then note any extenuating factors.

Total Stress Score: _____ = (Stress Score _____ – Coping Score _____)

Interpretation

Because this scale has not yet been "normed" on a large sample, the total stress score should be interpreted cautiously. Generally, we believe that a score of 20-30 should be a cause for concern, and a score above 30 should suggest immediate intervention to help a child deal with stress.

No matter what the score, it is important to help the child find ways to reduce stress in his/her life and seek developmentally-appropriate ways to handle the stresses that cannot be avoided or controlled.

Notes

#11 Classroom Modifications Checklist

Many ADHD children need specific classroom modifications in order to learn effectively. In fact, their right to receive such modifications, in the least restrictive environment possible, is guaranteed in Section 504 of the Federal Rehabilitation Act. The teacher can use the following checklist to make sure that all appropriate modifications are considered in planning the child's educational program.

Classroom Modifications Checklists

Directions: Check off appropriate modifications that will enhance the learning of the ADHD child.

1. _____ Study carrels
2. _____ Displaying classroom rules
3. _____ Posting daily schedule and homework assignments
4. _____ Planned methods for transitions between activities
5. _____ Seating the child in close proximity to the teacher
6. _____ Academic class assignments structured for times of maximum attention (i.e., usually the morning)
7. _____ Alternating types of work and using a multisensory approach
8. _____ Complex tasks broken down into steps that can be achieved
9. _____ Predictable routines and schedules
10. _____ Extended-time tests
11. _____ Tests in quiet environments
12. _____ Teacher checks organization of desk
13. _____ Teacher checks that homework assignments are recorded appropriately
14. _____ Behavioral point system
15. _____ Non-verbal or other cues are used to give the child appropriate behavioral feedback
16. _____ Structured and frequent home/school communication
17. _____ In-class tutoring (parent, other students, para-educators)
18. _____ Shortened or modified assignments
19. _____ Access to computers to carry out assignments
20. _____ Methods for recording homework assignments and organizing work area
21. _____ Teacher checks backpack of student at the end of the day to see that the appropriate books/materials are going home — Parent checks backpack before school in a.m. to see that books/materials/assignments are going back to school

_____ Other _____

_____ Other _____

_____ Other _____

Comments: _____

_____

_____

_____

#12 Daily Planner

Classroom routine is an important aspect of school that can affect an ADHD child's performance. Because they are so easily distracted, ADHD children need a highly-structured and organized environment. Teachers can increase children's cooperation by structuring a routine and preparing children carefully for transitions.

The **Daily Planner** can be an aid in planning a daily routine to facilitate learning for the ADHD child. Transitions can be listed, and the teacher's behavioral expectations should be made clear.

Daily Planner

Child's Name: _____

Day: _____

Classroom: _____

PERIOD

_____

_____

_____

_____

_____

_____

_____

_____

_____

ACTIVITY

_____

_____

_____

_____

_____

_____

_____

_____

_____

_____

TRANSITIONS

_____

_____

_____

_____

EXPECTATIONS

_____

_____

_____

_____

#13 Emotions Chart

Children with ADHD are characterized by emotional reactivity. Getting them to talk about their feelings is an important part of teaching them self-control.

In addition, ADHD children may have difficulty with their emotional reactions to adults and peers who may be critical and disapproving. The **Emotions Chart** is a first step in getting ADHD children to understand "negative" emotions and ways to handle them.

Emotions Chart

Fill in examples of the emotions below and possible things to do if someone feels the emotion.

FRUSTRATED

WHAT TO DO

EMBARRASSED

WHAT TO DO

SAD

WHAT TO DO

ANGRY

WHAT TO DO

ANXIOUS

WHAT TO DO

33

#14 Family Chores Chart

ADHD children often have difficulty being cooperative and/or responsible, but this may be due to unclear expectations and instructions. Learning to be a responsible and cooperative member of the family is important for all children, but ADHD children may need some extra help in making this contribution successfully.

The **Family Chores Chart** is designed to treat all members of the family equally, assigning each member a specific chore.

Family Chores Chart

At a family meeting, designate the week's chores for each family member (including adults). Enter the name of each person and each chore in the appropriate space. Enter the time and day that the chore is to be performed if appropriate. Enter a "+" if the chore is performed appropriately and a "–" if it is missed or not performed correctly. Problems should be discussed at the next family meeting.

NAME	CHORE	MON	TUES	WED	THURS	FRI	SAT	SUN

#15 Feelings Diary

ADHD children typically have a difficult time both communicating their feelings and understanding the feelings of others. Giving them the opportunity to think and talk about their feelings not only helps build a "feelings vocabulary," but also gives them a positive experience with a supportive adult, enhancing their confidence and self-esteem.

To be effective, the **Feelings Diary** should be filled out regularly. If every day is too often, then it might be done on two designated nights a week. Make copies of the Feelings Diary form, and keep the completed forms in a loose-leaf binder so that the diary can be read in its entirety at any time.

Feelings Diary

NAME: _____ DATE: _____

MY IMPORTANT FEELINGS TODAY WERE:

_____

_____

_____

_____

_____

OTHER FEELINGS I HAD TODAY WERE:

_____

_____

_____

_____

_____

FEELINGS I WOULD LIKE TO CHANGE ARE:

_____

_____

_____

_____

THIS IS HOW I WOULD CHANGE THEM:

_____

_____

_____

_____

#16 "Free Time" Chart

The way children spend their "free time" can have a tremendous influence on their social and emotional growth. Use this chart to go through a "typical" week with a child to get a sense of how much time is devoted to play, homework, chores, TV, religious instruction, and so on.

While older children can sometimes go through a daily schedule in their mind, younger children will reveal how they spend their time through direct questions. Use the following questions to elicit their sense of how they spend their time. Verify their answers with adults if there is concern.

Questions

1. When do you do your homework each day?
2. When do you watch TV each day?
3. What sports practice do you have?
4. Do you belong to any clubs? When do they meet?
5. Do you have religious instruction after school or on weekends?
6. What do you do most on Saturdays?
7. What do you do most on Sundays?
8. Do you take any lessons? When do you take them?
9. Do you have video or computer games at your house? When do you play them?
10. Does your family do things together? What are they? When do you do them?
11. Do you have any hobbies? When do you do them?
12. What chores do you have? When do you do them?
13. When do you play with your friends? What do you do?
14. What are some of your favorite things to do? When do you do them?
15. What things don't you like to do? When do you do them?

"Free Time" Chart

Name _____ Date Completed _____

HOURS	SUN	MON	TUE	WED	THURS	FRI	SAT
6AM							
7AM							
8AM							
9AM							
10AM							
11AM							
12Noon							
1PM							
2PM							
3PM							
4PM							
5PM							
6PM							
7PM							
8PM							
9PM							
10PM							
11PM							
12 Midnight							

#17 Frustration Tolerance Checklist

One of the most distinguishing characteristics of ADHD children is their lack of patience. Patience is somewhat different than impulsivity, although the two are obviously related. Patience has to do with the ability to tolerate frustration and delay gratification, while impulsivity usually refers to the child's propensity to act quickly without thinking or reflecting on the consequences. Theoretically it is easier to teach a child patience, which has to do with the inhibition of response, then to teach children to be less impulsive, which requires learning new cognitive mediating skills. The Frustration Tolerance Checklist was designed to identify areas where the child already shows age appropriate patience and to transfer these skills to other areas.

This checklist is written in positive behavioral terms and is designed so that it can easily be used as an assessment tool, to write behavioral objectives, and as a pre and post treatment measure.

Frustration Tolerance Checklist

Name of Child: _____

Date Filled Out: _____

Filled Out By: _____

Write in the appropriate number of minutes by each statement or check "not a problem."

Home	# of Minutes	Not a Problem
1. Waits in line without complaining.	_____	_____
2. Does homework without supervision.	_____	_____
3. Does independent academic school work without supervision.	_____	_____
4. Sits in restaurant without complaining.	_____	_____
5. Sits at home meals without getting up.	_____	_____
6. Plays board games with children of same age.	_____	_____
7. Listens to stories.	_____	_____
8. Reads books.	_____	_____
9. Works at a hobby.	_____	_____
10. Rides in car without complaining.	_____	_____
11. Works at puzzles.	_____	_____
12. Uses a computer.	_____	_____
13. Does chores without supervision.	_____	_____
14. Waits in a store (i.e. grocery) without complaining.	_____	_____
15. Takes care of personal hygiene without supervision.	_____	_____

Other:

_____ _____ _____

_____ _____ _____

_____ _____ _____

_____ _____ _____

#18 Goal Chart

When tasks are difficult, they must be broken into small sequential steps. The **Goal Chart** can be used to help children learn difficult or complicated tasks by mastering and being rewarded for small successes.

Goal Chart

Determine a general goal and objective and then divide that goal into sub-steps. When each step is accomplished, color in a football. When the last football is colored in, the overall goal is accomplished.

NAME _____

GOAL _____

DATE STARTED _____   DATE TO BE ACCOMPLISHED _____

STEPS:

1. _____

2. _____

3. _____

4. _____

5. _____

6. _____

7. _____

#19 Good Acts List

When children do good deeds, they incorporate a sense of themselves as "good" into their self-image. This is very significant for the ADHD child, who typically gets negative feedback from his or her environment.

Just as importantly, other people in the child's life will view and treat the ADHD differently as he or she performs kind, considerate, and helpful acts.

The **Good Acts List** should be filled out to help a child think of at least 12 things that he or she could do for someone else. Every week, the child should select from the list and then pick a time and place for the "good deed" to be accomplished. Following the act, the child should record his or her reactions and feelings about it.

Good Acts List

Act	What Happened?
1.	
2.	
3.	
4.	
5.	
6.	
7.	
8.	
9.	
10.	
11.	
12.	
13.	
14.	
15.	
16.	
17.	
18.	
19.	
20.	

#20 Good Listening Form And Score Card

The Good Listening Form was designed to help ADHD children practice Active Listening skills. Active Listening refers to a technique whereby the child shows the speaker that he is listening by paraphrasing what he/she has said. If the listener is not entirely correct, the speaker then must say what the listener left out or misunderstood. This form will help the child record and concentrate on what the speaker is saying.

The Listening Score Card is filled out by the speaker who rates the listener on Active Listening skills. A perfect score would be 6.

Good Listening Form and Score Card

1. **WRITE DOWN THE MAIN POINTS THAT YOU HEARD:**

   _____
   _____
   _____
   _____
   _____
   _____

2. **CIRCLE THE KEY WORDS OR CONCEPTS ABOVE.**

3. **WRITE DOWN ANYTHING THAT THE SPEAKER SAYS YOU MISSED.**

   _____
   _____
   _____
   _____
   _____
   _____

4. **WRITE DOWN THE MOST IMPORTANT THING THAT THE SPEAKER SAID:**

   _____
   _____
   _____
   _____
   _____
   _____

Listening Score Card

The Speaker should give the Listener one point for each statement that is true.

____ He/she watched me while I talked.

____ He/she did not interrupt me while I talked.

____ He/she did not fiddle or act impatient while I talked.

____ He/she seemed interested in what I was saying.

____ He/she repeated back the important points that I said.

____ He/she repeated back any additions or corrections that I made.

#21 Homework Completion Chart

Nearly every child can benefit from an organized schedule of homework. The **Homework Completion Chart** was designed to help parents plan the appropriate time to do homework and to monitor its completion.

Homework Completion Chart

NAME _____

WEEK OF _____

Assignments/ Subjects	MON			TUE			WED			THURS			FRI			SAT			SUN		
	TIME ___ TO ___	DONE	APPR. BY	TIME ___ TO ___	DONE	APPR. BY	TIME ___ TO ___	DONE	APPR. BY	TIME ___ TO ___	DONE	APPR. BY	TIME ___ TO ___	DONE	APPR. BY	TIME ___ TO ___	DONE	APPR. BY	TIME ___ TO ___	DONE	APPR. BY

#22 Learning Style Checklist

All teachers know that different children have different ways of learning. But this may be exaggerated in ADHD children. The Learning Style Checklist was designed to insure that a child is getting the most out of his/her education, by optimizing the way that information is presented, both in school and at home. This checklist should be filled in by the teacher or other trained observer, who has the opportunity to work the child in each of the different modalities.

Learning Style Checklist

Name of Child: _____

Name of Observer: _____

Date: _____

Directions: Rate each modality of learning on the 5 factors listed at the top of the page. using a 5 pt. rating scale. Total the numbers for each learning modality to compare the different ways that the child learns.

1 = Poor   2 = Fair   3 = Average   4 = Above Average   5 = Excellent

	Attentive	Motivated	Asks Questions	Retains Information	Seeks Information	TOTAL
Teacher Talking						
Peer Talking						
Group Work						
Written Work						
Art						
Dramatic Expression						
Computer						
Video/Movies						
Learning Board Games						
Flash Cards						
Others:						

#23 Making (Or Losing) Friends (Self Report Form)

Children with ADHD typically lack many of the skills that they need to make and keep friends. Social isolation and/or peer rejection can then become more troubling to the ADHD child than any of the true symptoms and will undoubtedly contribute to poor self-esteem.

The Making Friends Form was designed to help children learn that there are specific things that they can do to help them make and keep friends, and also that there are specific behaviors which keep them from forming friendships. This form can be used as part of a social skills training program for individuals or groups of children. It can be used as a way to spark conversation, or as a way to record behaviors both in the therapy sessions as well as in day to day life.

The Making (or Losing) Friends Form

Name _____ Date _____

Directions: Check each statement that applies to you today. Try to do more things to make friends and less things to lose friends everyday.

Things I did today to help make friends:

1. _____ I offered help to someone else.
2. _____ I smiled when I passed someone.
3. _____ I said 'hello' to people that I knew.
4. _____ I looked at people directly when they spoke.
5. _____ I used good manners when I met new people.
6. _____ I asked someone to play with me.
7. _____ I said something nice to someone that I like.
8. _____ I listened quietly when someone was talking.
9. _____ I shared something I had with someone else.
10. _____ I asked someone what they wanted to do.
11. _____ I saw other kids playing and asked if I could join them.
12. _____ I did my work quietly without bothering any one.
13. _____ I followed class rules
14. _____ I complimented someone and really meant it.
15. _____ I called someone at home.
16. _____ I invited someone over to play.
17. _____ I became interested in something new that someone else told me about.
18. _____ I thought of a new game or activity and played it with someone.
19. _____ I included someone new in a game or activity.
20. _____ I did something nice for someone, just because I felt like it.

Other Things I Did:

_____
_____
_____
_____
_____

Things I did today to lose friends:

1. _____ I changed the topic when someone was talking.
2. _____ I was a tattle tale.
3. _____ I whined about things I didn't like.
4. _____ I cheated at a game.
5. _____ I interrupted someone.
6. _____ I played too rough.
7. _____ I was rude.
8. _____ I teased someone.
9. _____ I didn't listen when someone else was talking.
10. _____ I sat by myself at lunch and didn't talk to anyone.
11. _____ I wouldn't share something I had.
12. _____ I wouldn't let others share in what I was doing.
13. _____ I was in a bad mood and told people to get away.
14. _____ I played too silly for other people.
15. _____ I wouldn't do what someone else wanted.
16. _____ I watched TV or played video games in all my free time.
17. _____ I didn't feel like talking to anyone.
18. _____ I told a lie or fib about someone.
19. _____ I ignored someone that I didn't like.
20. _____ I said something mean to someone to hurt their feelings.

Other Things I Did:

_____
_____
_____
_____
_____

#24 Manners (Self-Monitoring) Checklist

Many ADHD children are perceived as difficult by teachers and other adults, and in fact ADHD children typically lack the social skills that adults value. While it is not realistic to expect ADHD children to change their personalities to be more "likable," it is possible to teach specific social skills, including manners, which are highly regarded by adults.

It is presumed that if children develop better manners then they will be perceived as more socially appropriate by adults, and will in return receive more positive attention and reinforcement.

The Manners Checklist is designed to be a simple way in which children can learn and self-monitor their polite behavior. Children give themselves points for their good manners, which can then be acknowledged or rewarded by an adult supervising the child's treatment program. Groups of children can play a game and see how many "manners points" they can collect in one day.

Manners Checklist

Name _____

Date _____

Directions: Manners are very important to adults. Give yourself a check mark, each time you do any of the things listed below. See how many points you can get in just one day!

1.   I smiled at someone and said hello.   _____

2.   I said "please" when I asked for something.   _____

3.   I said "thank you" when I got something.   _____

4.   I used good table manners.   _____

5.   I paid attention when someome was talking.   _____

6.   I did something for someone else without being asked.   _____

7.   I let someone go ahead of me.   _____

8.   I said "excuse me" if I did something that was rude.   _____

9.   I apologized if I did something wrong.   _____

10.   I asked before I used something that didn't belong to me.   _____

11.   I didn't complain about something I didn't like.   _____

12.   I waited patiently.   _____

13.   I asked to be excused when I wanted to leave the table.   _____

14.   I didn't talk out of turn.   _____

15.   I didn't interrupt anyone.   _____

#25 Menu of Rewards

When rewarding a child for good behavior, adults should be sure the reward is something they can realistically provide. It is helpful for the child to choose the reward with the adult. Rewards should be tangible, such as a small toy, activities, or privileges. It should be something extra, rather than something the child would get anyway. Rewards should not be allowance money or time spent with friends.

The **Menu of Rewards** will help in choosing an appropriate reward for a behavioral program.

Menu Of Rewards

FILL IN THE NUMBER OF POINTS NEEDED TO RECEIVE ONE OF THE FOLLOWING REWARDS:

POINTS

_____ GETTING A HUG
_____ FOOD TREAT
_____ SMALL TOY/PRIZE
_____ PLAYING A GAME _____
_____ ACTIVITY _____ _____ (WITH WHOM?)
      (WHAT KIND?)
_____ TV TIME
_____ SPECIAL DINNER
_____ MONEY $
_____ GOING TO A RESTAURANT _____
_____ MOVIE _____
_____ VIDEO _____
_____ OTHERS:

_____ _____ _____ _____ _____

NAME _____

DATE _____

57

#26 Monthly Graph

The **Monthly Graph** can be used to plot daily points earned over a month's period. Drawing a graph of points earned can help show important patterns as well as progress.

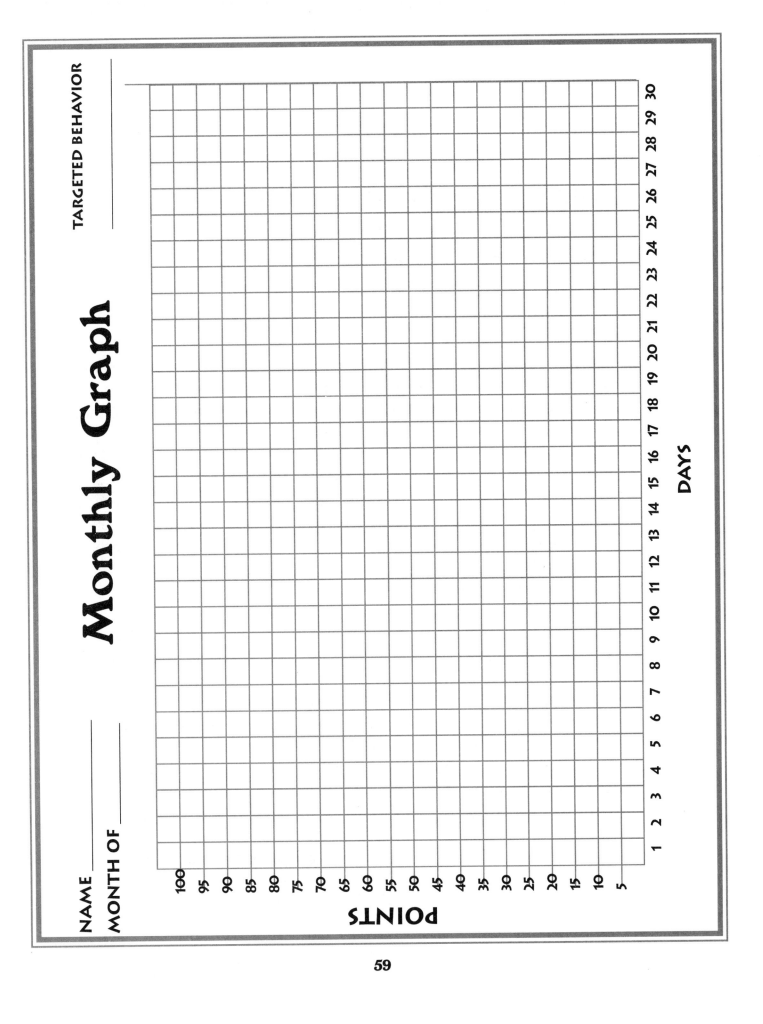

Monthly Graph

NAME _____
MONTH OF _____

TARGETED BEHAVIOR
_____

POINTS

100
95
90
85
80
75
70
65
60
55
50
45
40
35
30
25
20
15
10
5

DAYS

1 2 3 4 5 6 7 8 9 10 11 12 13 14 15 16 17 18 19 20 21 22 23 24 25 26 27 28 29 30

#27 Oppositional Behavior Checklist (Form A: Children's Checklist)
#28 Oppositional Behavior Checklist (Form B: Adult Checklist)

A therapist or counselor always hopes that the children that they treat or the parents or teachers that they work with will cooperate with the treatment program. But unfortunately that is not always the case. Many children, as well as adults, have oppositional characteristics to their personality, and whether they are aware of it or not, they fight against the therapist's best intentions.

When faced with oppositional personalities, the therapist can either try a rational approach, pointing out how people may be working against their own best interest, or they can try an "oppositional approach" where they actually use the person's oppositionality as a way to get them to cooperate. With either approach, the therapist must be able to distinguish positive attributes of the oppositional character from attributes which are self-defeating.

The Oppositional Behavior Checklist has two forms: one for children and one for adults. Each form consists of statements which the person can rate using a three point scale. The odd numbered statements consist of behaviors that could be due to oppositional personality traits, but could also be viewed as positive attributes, including independence, assertiveness, and so on. The even numbered statements describe oppositional traits which are self-defeating and/or break acceptable rules or ethical standards. It is important for the therapist or counselor to distinguish these two types of behavior in order to guide the child or adult towards the therapeutic goal while utilizing their personality strengths.

Each form has two totals. Total I is for the even numbered statements, and Total II is for the odd numbered statements.

Oppositional Behavior Checklist

FORM A: CHILDREN'S CHECKLIST

Name _____   Date _____

Please rate the following on a 3 point scale:
1 = Always   2 = Sometimes   3 = Never

1. _____ Would you say "no" to someone who wanted you to do something that was bad for you?

2. _____ Do you ever lie about something you did?

3. _____ Would you work to make money if your parents wouldn't buy you something that you wanted?

4. _____ Do you ever cut class?

5. _____ Would you say something to your parents if they were smoking cigarettes?

6. _____ Do you ever say you will run away from home because you are mad?

7. _____ Would you say something to someone who was driving without a seat belt?

8. _____ Do you ever throw something when you are really angry?

9. _____ Would you tell the teacher if someone was calling you names?

10. _____ Do you ever talk back to your teacher?

11. _____ Would you say something to someone who butted in line in front of you?

12. _____ Do you ever fight over the TV?

13. _____ Would you talk back to someone who was teasing you?

14. _____ Do you get into arguments with your friends?

15. _____ Would you stay home if you knew your friends were out looking for trouble?

16. _____ Do you ever skip doing your homework because you are too busy?

17. _____ Would you tell your parents if you thought they were doing something that was bad for you or someone else?

18. _____ Do you ever take things that don't belong to you?

19. _____ If you saw a younger child watching an "adult" show on TV would you turn it off or change the channel?

20. _____ Do you ever tease your brother or sister or other children?

TOTAL 1 _____   TOTAL 2 _____

Oppositional Behavior Checklist

FORM B: ADULT CHECKLIST

Name _____ Date _____

Please rate the following on a 3 point scale:
1 = Always   2 = Sometimes   3 = Never

1. _____ Would you say something if someone cut in front of you in line at the movies?
2. _____ Would you cheat on your taxes if you were positive that you wouldn't get caught?
3. _____ Do you speed if you don't think you will be caught?
4. _____ Would you complain to your child's teacher if you thought that she was doing something wrong?
5. _____ Would you leave without paying a bill at the restaurant if you had very bad service?
6. _____ Would you say something if you were overcharged on a restaurant bill by one dollar?
7. _____ Would you ignore your doctor's advice, even if you knew it was good?
8. _____ Would you write a letter to a store that gave you bad service?
9. _____ Would you tell your child's school that he/she was sick if you just wanted to keep him home for a day?
10. _____ Would you complain to the school principal if you child's teacher wouldn't listen to your concerns?
11. _____ Would you leave work early if you could get away with it?
12. _____ Would you go to court to fight a traffic ticket that you thought was unjustly given?
13. _____ Would you stop talking to someone that you were mad at?
14. _____ Would you take a boss to a hearing if you thought that he/she was harassing you?
15. _____ Would you try and "get even" with someone who you thought had done something you didn't like?
16. _____ Would you take back a product that you bought if you thought it was misrepresented?
17. _____ Would you send an angry letter to someone, even though you knew it would be hurtful and probably not help your relationship?
18. _____ Would you yell back at someone who was yelling at you for an argument that they started?
19. _____ Would you hang up the phone on someone you cared about, because they said something that made you mad?
20. _____ Would you call up your neighbor if their dog was barking every night?

TOTAL 1 _____   TOTAL 2 _____

63

#29 Organization Checklist

Many treatment programs for ADHD stress the need for organization and structure in a child's life. The following checklist can be used to help parents provide this organization, both in terms of place and time. The parent can use this form to identify areas that need more organization.

Organization Checklist

Name of Child: _____

Filled Out By: _____

Date: _____

Bedroom

_____ Closet
_____ Drawers
_____ Toys
_____ Work Materials

_____ _____
_____ _____

Study Area

_____ Desk
_____ Books
_____ Computer Area
_____ Homework

_____ _____
_____ _____

Bathroom

_____ Toothbrush And Toothpaste
_____ Shampoo
_____ Soap
_____ Medicines

_____ _____
_____ _____

Household Routine

_____ Wake-Up Time
_____ Bedtime
_____ Getting Ready For School
_____ Meals
_____ Chores
_____ Homework Time

_____ _____
_____ _____

Free Time

_____ TV Restriction
_____ Sports
_____ After School Time
_____ Weekends
_____ Hobbies

_____ _____
_____ _____

Organizing Materials

_____ Daily Planner
_____ Calendar
_____ Book Bag

_____ _____
_____ _____

#30 Parent Involvement Checklist

The majority of treatment programs used with ADHD children include some form of parent training. This can range from parent education, to discipline training, to a highly-structured training program.

There are many factors to consider in assessing the parent's willingness and ability to participate in a therapy program. In general, parents with high levels of stress and/or marital discord are not good candidates to be active participants in the child's therapy. On the other hand, a critical attitude toward the child or harsh discipline techniques by the parent is not necessarily a detriment to parent involvement in the therapy. A parent's strong emotional involvement with the child, even a negative one, may be a sign of caring. Obviously, parents who are abusive, either physically or verbally, are questionable candidates in aiding the therapeutic program of a child, and will often need intensive treatment for themselves.

Aside from a general willingness to participate in a treatment program and a respect for the therapist's expertise, time spent in basic child care activities is one of the best predictors of a parent's successful involvement in the therapy program. The **Parent Involvement Checklist** can be used to ascertain the past and present positive involvement that a parent, or parent surrogate, has had with the ADHD child.

Parent Involvement Checklist

Child's Name: _____

Parent's Name: _____

Presenting Problem: _____

Date: _____

Please check the following statements that are entirely true.

___ I tuck my child into bed every night.

___ I participated in toilet training my child.

___ I take my child to weeknight activities.

___ I take my child to weekend activities.

___ I read to my child at least once a week.

___ I play sports with my child at least once a week.

___ I participate in a hobby with my child at least once a week.

___ I take my child shopping with me.

___ I participate in school activities _____ times a month.

___ I participate in community-related activities with my child ___ a month
     (e.g., Scout Leader).

___ I watch TV with my child.

___ I help my child with homework on a regular basis.

___ I participate in sports or other physical activities with my child.

___ I play board games with my child at least once a week.

___ I have read a book related to child-rearing in the last month.

(Please list): _____

List other "nonessential"* activities that you do with your child on a regular basis.

_____

_____

_____

_____

_____

_____

*Nonessential activities are defined as activities that are not required for the child's basic health and well-being.

#31 Paying Attention Form

The **Paying Attention** Form can be used by a student to monitor his or her "attending" or "on-task" behavior. The adult should fill in the times that "attending" is important. Times can be entered in small increments (e.g., five minutes) for high-attention work or for longer increments (e.g., one hour) for tasks where attention needs to be less concentrated. Either the child or the adult can put a "+" for times when attention is appropriate and a "-" for times when the child is inattentive.

Paying Attention

TIME OF ACTIVITIES	MON	TUES	WED	THURS	FRI

NAME _____ WEEK OF _____ TOTAL SCORE _____

69

#32 Positive & Negative Self-Talk Form

A simple but effective strategy used to help ADHD children with a low self-esteem is teaching them to make positive rather than negative statements to themselves.

Some children who have been raised in an atmosphere of criticism (whether it is justified criticism or not) will frequently internalize negative things that adults say and begin saying those same things to themselves. Other children, who might have a very positive environment, will say negative things to themselves because they feel they are not good enough (smart enough, pretty enough, coordinated enough, etc.) according to the criteria by which they perceive the culture or their peers judge them.

The technique of teaching children to "think more positively" can be introduced by explaining how many professional athletes and entertainment stars use this technique to improve their performances. The following form can be used to help children list the "negative" things that they say to themselves and then substitute "positive self-talk"– positive and realistic attributes, abilities, attitudes, experiences, resources, etc.

The therapist or counselor will usually have to give one or two examples to help the child get started, such as:

When I was your age, I was very chubby. I used to get teased by other children, and I used to think that nobody liked me. I would think,

"Nobody likes me because I am fat."

But eventually I found friends who liked me because they thought I was fun to be with and we had things in common that we liked to do together. I was really good at bowling, and my friends and I formed a bowling club. I learned to say to myself, "I am really good at some things, like bowling and writing, and math. I can find friends who will like to do things that I like to do."

In drawing experiences from your own life, it is always important to be truthful. Try to pick something from your childhood that parallels your client's problem(s), while being judiciously honest. Naturally, do not disclose examples from your life that would not be helpful for the child to know.

The second part of learning to think more positively is believing in these thoughts. An additional column is furnished for the child to rate his/her belief in the thought: 1=Do not really believe; 10=Believe completely. When this technique is first used, the child will typically have a stronger belief in the negative rather than the positive thought. In the final column, the counselor should help the child list things that he/she can do that will support the positive statements. As children experience these things, the rating of the child's belief in the negative statements should go down and the rating of the positive statements should go up.

Positive and Negative Self-Talk Form

NEGATIVE THOUGHTS	BELIEF (1-10)	POSITIVE THOUGHTS	BELIEF (1-10)	EXPERIENCES TO SUPPORT POSITIVE THOUGHTS
1.				1.
2.				2.
3.				3.
4.				4.
5.				5.

#33 Preventive Intervention Chart

Preventive Intervention is a method of behavioral management that focuses on preventing misbehavior before it happens. This can be accomplished either through teaching the child skills for good behavior or through controlling the environment in such a way that specific misbehaviors are impossible to commit.

The **Preventive Intervention Chart** can aid in determining appropriate ways to educate the child and/or change the environment.

Preventive Intervention Chart

Name of child:_____ Date: _____

Filled out by: _____

INAPPROPRIATE BEHAVIOR	WAYS TO EDUCATE CHILD	WAYS TO CHANGE ENVIRONMENT
1.		
2.		
3.		
4.		
5.		

#34 Problem-Solving Steps Chart

All ADHD children can benefit by practicing problem-solving skills. Adults must take time to teach children sequential problem-solving steps by rehearsing these steps using problem situations that are meaningful to the child. Then the problem-solving steps must used at times when the ADHD child has specific problems or concerns, reinforcing each step to an appropriate solution.

PROBLEM-SOLVING STEPS CHART

Identify the problem:_____
What does this problem require me to do?
_____
_____

Three strategies for solving the problem:

Strategy #1

Step 1:	
Step 2:	
Step 3:	
Step 4:	

Strategy #2

Step 1:	
Step 2:	
Step 3:	
Step 4:	

Strategy #3

Step 1:	
Step 2:	
Step 3:	
Step 4:	

The Best Strategy Is: _____

#35 Rules Certificate

Use this **Rules Certificate** to display the rules that have been mastered. It should be posted in a prominent place to remind the child of his or her progress.

Rules
Certificate

I Have Mastered These Rules!

1. _____

_____

2. _____

_____

3. _____

_____

4. _____

_____

5. _____

_____

Child's Name_____ Date_____

Parent's Signature_____

#1

#36 Rules Form

Adults should implement rules of conduct to help govern and control a child's problematic behaviors. Significant elements of implementing rules include (1) start off with one or two rules; (2) be clear, concise, and specific; (3) include the consequence for infractions; (4) post the rules in a prominent location; and (5) respond to significant behaviors.

Use the **Rules Form** to keep a record of the rule that the child is currently trying to learn and track the child's success in learning that rule. When compliance is consistent for about a week (about 80% without reminders), the rule can be considered to have been learned.

Rules Form

Name:_____

Date:_____

Rule:_____

Consequence for Infraction:_____

Check One Column for Each Day	Compliance	Noncompliance	Compliance with Reminders
Sunday			
Monday			
Tuesday			
Wednesday			
Thursday			
Friday			
Saturday			

#37 School Behavior Progress Chart

There are many ways to measure behavioral progress of the ADHD child in school, but all methods should take into consideration the time involved for the teacher. Taking a time sample of behavior, three or four times during the day, is usually easier than keeping a behavioral chart going all day.

The teacher should select three or four 15-minute periods in which to rate specific objectives on a 1 to 5 scale. These periods should include one behavior that is difficult for the child, one with behavioral objectives that are usually easy for the child to meet, and one in between. The teacher should then rate the child during these periods, awarding points for improving behavior.

School Behavior Progress Chart

Name _____ Date _____

Circle the number that best describes the behavior in each period.
1=Inappropriate Behavior   5=Perfect Behavior

Period 1	Behavioral Objectives	Rating
	1._____	1 2 3 4 5
	2._____	1 2 3 4 5
	3._____	1 2 3 4 5
	4._____	1 2 3 4 5
	5._____	1 2 3 4 5
Period 2	Behavioral Objectives	Rating
	1._____	1 2 3 4 5
	2._____	1 2 3 4 5
	3._____	1 2 3 4 5
	4._____	1 2 3 4 5
	5._____	1 2 3 4 5
Period 3	Behavioral Objectives	Rating
	1._____	1 2 3 4 5
	2._____	1 2 3 4 5
	3._____	1 2 3 4 5
	4._____	1 2 3 4 5
	5._____	1 2 3 4 5
Period 4	Behavioral Objectives	Rating
	1._____	1 2 3 4 5
	2._____	1 2 3 4 5
	3._____	1 2 3 4 5
	4._____	1 2 3 4 5
	5._____	1 2 3 4 5
	Total for Day	_____

#38 Self-Monitoring Chart

Children with ADHD typically have difficulty in judging their own behavior. Specifically, they lack the self-observing and self-regulating capacities that would be expected of children the same age. An important goal of any behavior program is to teach children to monitor their behavior and take responsibility for changing it.

The **Self-Monitoring Chart** can be used to help children monitor a single important rule. The adult should select a period when or an activity in which the rule is particularly important. The adult should then give the child cues (such as raising a finger) at random intervals during that period. The child should mark down if he/she is following the rule when the cue is given.

Self-Monitoring Chart

My Behavior

Name: _____ Date: _____	Follow Rule (✔)	Not Follow Rule (✔)
Period or Activity: _____ Teacher: _____ Rule: _____		
Period or Activity: _____ Teacher: _____ Rule: _____		
Period or Activity: _____ Teacher: _____ Rule: _____		
Period or Activity: _____ Teacher: _____ Rule: _____		
Period or Activity: _____ Teacher: _____ Rule: _____		
	Total	Total

#39 Side Effects Checklist

Research has established the short-term effectiveness of stimulant medication in improving the symptoms of ADHD. Common side effects, such as loss of appetite and insomnia, are usually mild and resolve spontaneously with a decrease in dosage. Some researchers are concerned about the long-term side effects of stimulant medication, including the suppression of height and weight gain as well as the development of the cardiovascular system. However, to date studies suggest that long-term effects may be mild. It is important to note, however, that about 1% of children will develop a tic disorder as a response to stimulant medication and that in some cases this may be irreversible. It is important in a medical intervention to constantly monitor and determine the presence of side effects, and the **Side Effects Checklist** can be used for this purpose.

SIDE EFFECTS CHECKLIST

Child's Name _____

Rater's Name _____

Date _____

Date of last rating _____

The following are some common side effects of psychostimulant medication. Many of these improve with the passage of time or with a change in dosage. Rate the presence of each symptom below.

Loss of Appetite	None 1 2 3 4 5 Severe
Insomnia	None 1 2 3 4 5 Severe
Sadness	None 1 2 3 4 5 Severe
Depression	None 1 2 3 4 5 Severe
Fearfulness	None 1 2 3 4 5 Severe
Social Withdrawal	None 1 2 3 4 5 Severe
Sleepiness	None 1 2 3 4 5 Severe
Headaches	None 1 2 3 4 5 Severe
Nail Biting	None 1 2 3 4 5 Severe
Stomach Upset	None 1 2 3 4 5 Severe
Weight Loss	None 1 2 3 4 5 Severe
Irritability	None 1 2 3 4 5 Severe
Tics	None 1 2 3 4 5 Severe
Behavior Seems Worse When Off Medication	None 1 2 3 4 5 Severe
Anxiety	None 1 2 3 4 5 Severe

Comments:

#40 Social Skills Assessment Form

Many ADHD children have problems in social skills. In the classroom and on the playground, they can be scapegoats and the objects of teasing and cruelty. Many ADHD children cannot maintain intimate friendships. Feelings of rejection decrease their motivation and self-esteem.

Improving social skills and working toward increasing social status will help a child's self image. Use the **Social Skills Assessment Form** to decide which social skills you want to target with a particular child. Rate the child according to his or her ability at each particular social skill. Prioritize the listed skills and work on only one or two at a time.

Social Skills Assessment Form

Circle the appropriate number by each social skill.

SKILL	ABILITY	DON'T KNOW
	ADEPT DEFICIENT	
Introducing self to others	5 4 3 2 1	DK
Entering a conversation	5 4 3 2 1	DK
Listening without interrupting	5 4 3 2 1	DK
Making eye contact	5 4 3 2 1	DK
Ending a conversation	5 4 3 2 1	DK
Following directions	5 4 3 2 1	DK
Offering help	5 4 3 2 1	DK
Sharing	5 4 3 2 1	DK
Accepting responsibility for actions	5 4 3 2 1	DK
Asking for help	5 4 3 2 1	DK
Compromising	5 4 3 2 1	DK
Ignoring teasing and provocation	5 4 3 2 1	DK
Joining a group	5 4 3 2 1	DK
Following rules of play	5 4 3 2 1	DK
Handling peer pressure	5 4 3 2 1	DK
Expressing own emotions	5 4 3 2 1	DK
Expressing own opinions	5 4 3 2 1	DK
Handling anger	5 4 3 2 1	DK
Handling failure	5 4 3 2 1	DK
Handling other people's anger	5 4 3 2 1	DK
Handling success	5 4 3 2 1	DK
Speaking in a pleasant tone of voice	5 4 3 2 1	DK
Speaking at an appropriate rate	5 4 3 2 1	DK
Using appropriate body language	5 4 3 2 1	DK

#41 "Special Time" Recording Form

Special Time refers to a 15 to 30 minute period of time when the parent or another concerned person plays with the ADHD child demonstrating unconditional acceptance. Most therapists agree that this form of play therapy is very important for children with behavior problems, because it builds a bond between the parents and children, aids in communication, and enhances their self-esteem. The principles of Special Time are easy to teach to parents, and include:

• Praising the child for positive attributes and behavior.
• Reflecting back what the child says.
• Participating in the play in a way which mirrors the child's interests.
• Refraining from being judgmental or critical.
• Setting clear limits for when the play starts and stops.

The Special Time Recording Form will help parents remember to do this activity regularly and keep track of the child's interests and feelings.

"Special Time" Recording Form

Name of Child: _____

Name of Parent: _____

DATE	START TIME	END TIME	ACTIVITY	CHILD'S COMMENTS	OBSERVATIONS

#42 Teacher-Parent Progress Card

Cooperation between parents and teachers can be one of the most important determinants of a successful treatment program for the ADHD child. In some systems, the teacher sends a note to the parents every day. The note can state how the child behaved that day and how he or she did with homework. It can also list upcoming homework and furnish warnings for upcoming projects.

The **Teacher-Parent Progress Card** can be used for communication between parent and teacher. Parents should always ask the child for the card. If the adults feel that the child is progressing, they can use the card once a week instead of every day.

Teacher-Parent Progress Card

Child's Name: _____ Date: _____

Teacher: _____

PREVIOUS DAY'S HOMEWORK:

Neatness _____

Completion _____

Accuracy _____

BEHAVIOR _____

_____

_____

TONIGHT'S HOMEWORK _____

_____

UPCOMING PROJECTS _____

_____

COMMENTS: _____

_____

_____

_____

_____

#43 Time-Out Worksheet

Prior to implementing a time-out strategy, the adult and child should discuss (1) what time-out is and (2) for which behaviors time-out will be used. The adult should be specific and thorough so that the child clearly understands the consequences that will follow misbehavior. The **Time-Out Worksheet** can be used to organize and record a time-out plan.

Time-Out Worksheet

Name of Child_____

Age of Child_____

Length of Time-Out_____Minutes (1 minute for each year of child's age)

Location of Time-Out Center_____

Behavior to Regulate: (Pick 1 to 3 specific problematic behaviors)

1. _____

2. _____

3. _____

Record the number of time-outs given in a week:

Problem Behavior	Day	Time	Child's Attitude

#44 Token Economy Chart

A token economy system is a method of positive reinforcement that encourages a child to (1) increase the frequency of engaging in specific positive behaviors or (2) replace specific incidents of poor behavior with more desirable ones.

The **Token Economy Chart** should clearly state the behaviors that are to be reinforced and rewards that can accompany them by week's end. Children can receive tokens (such as poker chips) or stickers, and this should be noted on the chart. The chart should be posted in a highly-visible area so that the child can see how many tokens (or stickers) have been accumulated and how many are needed to earn the desired reward.

Token Economy Chart

Child's Name_____ Week Beginning_____

Day	Behavior(s)	Tokens Earned
Monday	1. 2. 3.	
Tuesday	1. 2. 3.	
Wednesday	1. 2. 3.	
Thursday	1. 2. 3.	
Friday	1. 2. 3.	
Saturday	1. 2. 3.	
Sunday	1. 2. 3.	

TOTAL: _____

Reward to Be Earned: _____

Points Needed: _____

#45 Weekly Graph

Graphs can be an important visual aid to help children and adults see progress or problems. The **Weekly Graph** can be used to track the daily points earned on up to three behavioral objectives.

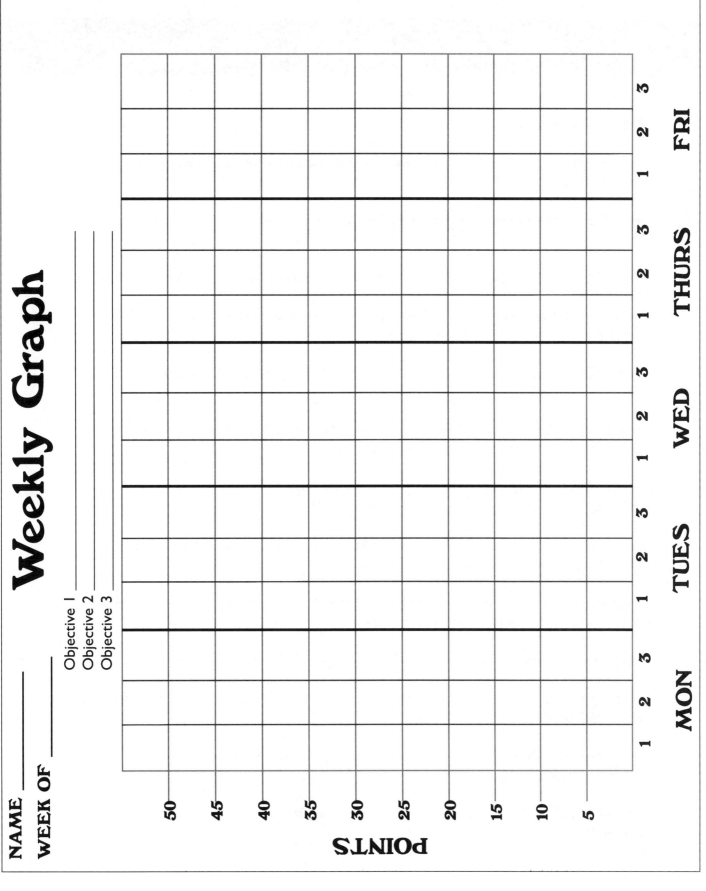

Weekly Graph

NAME _____

WEEK OF _____

Objective 1 _____
Objective 2 _____
Objective 3 _____

POINTS

50
45
40
35
30
25
20
15
10
5

1 2 3	1 2 3	1 2 3	1 2 3	1 2 3
MON	TUES	WED	THURS	FRI

97

Selected Bibliography and Resources

Reference Books

The Hyperactivity Workbook for Parents, Teachers, and Kids by Harvey C. Parker (Plantation, FL: Impact Publications, 1988).

The ADD Hyperactivity Handbook for Schools by Harvey C. Parker (Plantation, FL: Impact Publications, 1992).

ADHD/Hyperactivity: A Consumer's Guide by M. Gordon (DeWitt, NY: GSI Publications, 1991).

ADHD in the Schools: Assessment and Intervention Strategies by George J. DuPaul and Gary Stoner (New York, NY: Guilford Press, 1994).

Attention Deficit Hyperactivity Disorder: A Clinical Workbook by Russell A. Barkley (New York, NY: Guilford Press, 1990).

Attention Deficit Hyperactivity Disorder: A Handbook for Diagnosis and Treatment by Russell A. Barkley (New York, NY: Guilford Press, 1990).

Attention Deficit Hyperactivity Disorder: Questions and Answers for Parents by Gregory Greenberg and Wade Horn (Champaign, IL: Research Press, 1991).

Disruptive Behavior Disorders in Children by Michael Breen and Thomas Altpeter (New York, NY: Guilford Press, 1990).

Dr. Larry Silver's Advice to Parents on Attention-Deficit Hyperactivity Disorder by Larry B. Silver (Washington, DC: American Psychiatric Press, 1993).

Help for the Hyperactive Child by William G. Crook (Jackson, TN: Professional Books, 1991).

How to Reach and Teach ADD/ADHD Children by Sandra F. Reif (West Nyack, NY: The Center for Applied Research, 1993).

The Hyperactive Child, Adolescent, and Adult by Paul H. Wender (New York, NY: Oxford University Press, 1987).

Hyperactive Children Grown Up by Gabrielle Weiss and Lily T. Hechtman (New York, NY: Guilford Press, 1993).

Hyperactivity, the So-Called Attention-Deficit Disorder, and the Group of MBD Syndromes by Richard Gardner (Cresskill, NJ: Creative Therapeutics, 1987).

Hyperactivity: Why Won't My Child Pay Attention? by Sam Goldstein and Michael Goldstein (New York, NY: John Wiley, 1992).

If Your Child is Hyperactive, Impulsive, Distractible... by Stephen Garber, Marianne D. Garber and Robyn F. Spizman (New York, NY: Villard Books, 1990).

Managing Attention Disorders in Children: A Guide for Practitioners by Sam Goldstein and Michael Goldstein (New York, NY: John Wiley & Sons, 1990).

Maybe You Know My Kid: A Parents' Guide to Identifying, Understanding, and Helping Your Child with ADHD by Mary Fowler (New York, NY: Birch Lane Press, 1993).

Parenting the Overactive Child by Paul Lavin (Lanham, MD: Madison Books, 1989).

The Parents' Hyperactivity Handbook by David M. Paltin (New York, NY; Insight Books, 1993).

Sometimes I Get All Scribbly; Living with Attention Deficit Hyperactivity Disorder by Maureen Neuville (La Crosse, WI: Crystal Press, 1991).

Why Johnny Can't Concentrate: Coping with Attention Deficit Problems by Robert Moss (New York, NY: Bantam Books, 1990).

Your Hyperactive Child: A Parent's Guide to Coping with Attention Deficit Disorder by Barbara Ingersoll (New York, NY: Main Street Books, 1988).

Books for Children

Eagle Eyes: A Child's Guide to Paying Attention by Jeanne Gehret (Fairport: Verbal Images Press, 1991).

Putting On the Brakes: Young Peoples' Guide to Understanding ADHD by Patricia O. Quinn and Judith M. Stern (New York, NY: Magination Press, 1991).

Jumpin' Jake Settles Down: A Workbook to Help Impulsive Children Learn to Think Before They Act by Lawrence E. Shapiro (Secaucus, NJ: Childswork/Childsplay, 1994).

Learning to Slow Down and Pay Attention by Kathleen Nadeau and Ellen Dixon (Annandale, VA: Chesapeake Psychological Publications, 1993).

Otto Learns About His Medicine by M. Galvin (New York, NY: Magination Press, 1988).

Putting on the Brakes by Patricia O. Quinn and Judith M. Stern (New York, NY: Magination Press, 1992).

Shelley the Hyperactive Turtle by D. Moss (Rockville, MD: Woodbine House, 1989).

Sometimes I Drive My Mom Crazy, But I Know She's Crazy About Me: A Self-Esteem Book for ADHD Children by Lawrence E. Shapiro (King of Prussia, PA: The Center for Applied Psychology, Inc., 1993).

Videotapes

ADHD in Adults featuring Russell A. Barkley (New York, NY: Guilford Press, 1994).

ADHD in the Classroom featuring Russell A. Barkley (New York, NY: Guilford Press, 1994).

ADHD What Do We Know? featuring Russell A. Barkley (New York, NY: Guilford Press, 1992).

ADHD What Can We Do? featuring Russell A. Barkley (New York, NY: Guilford Press, 1992).

Educating Inattentive Children featuring Sam Goldstein and Michael Goldstein (Salt Lake City, UT: Neurology, Learning and Behavior Center,).

Why Won't My Child Pay Attention? featuring Sam Goldstein (Salt Lake City, UT: Neurology, Learning and Behavior Center).

Games

Stop, Relax and Think! by Childswork/Childsplay (Secaucus, NJ: 1991).

Look Before You Leap! by Childswork/Childsplay (Secaucus, NJ: 1994).